Dolores Huerta

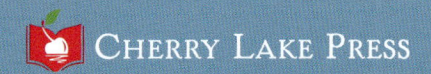

CHERRY LAKE PRESS

Published in the United States of America by Cherry Lake Publishing
Ann Arbor, Michigan
www.cherrylakepublishing.com

Reading Adviser: Beth Walker Gambro, MS, Ed., Reading Consultant, Yorkville, IL
Illustrator: Leo Trinidad

Photo Credits: © NMHM/DCA, 5; © Jacob Boomsma / Shutterstock, 7; © John Kouns, Courtesy of the Tom & Ethel Bradley Center at California State University, Northridge, 9; Courtesy of The Bob Fitch Photography Archive, Standford University Libraries, 11; Clarke, Emmon/ Bradley Center / CSUN University Library, 13; Walter P. Reuther collection, Wayne State University via the Smithsonian Institution, 15, 22; John Malmin, Los Angeles Times, UCLA via Wikimedia Commons CC BY SA 4.0, 17; © UPI / Alamy Stock Photo, 19, 23; Rafa213 via Wikimedia Commons CC BY SA 4.0, 21

Copyright © 2025 by Cherry Lake Publishing
All rights reserved. No part of this book may be reproduced or utilized in any form or by any means without written permission from the publisher.

Cherry Lake Press is an imprint of Cherry Lake Publishing Group

Library of Congress Cataloging-in-Publication Data has been filed and is available at catalog.loc.gov.

Printed in the United States of America

About the author: Brenda Perez Mendoza is an award-winning educator and the author of the Racial Justice in America: Latinx American series. She grew up in Cicero, Illinois, as a native language Spanish speaker. When she went to school, there wasn't enough support for students learning the English language. That is what drove her to become a K–12 ELL specialist and work with bilingual students. She works to advocate for all students, Latinx especially, to embrace their culture and celebrate who they are. Today, she lives in Chicago, Illinois, and is committed to providing students with culturally responsive practices and advocating for the whole child.

About the illustrator: Leo Trinidad is a NY Times bestselling comic book artist, illustrator, and animator from Costa Rica. For more than 12 years he's been creating content for children's books and TV shows. Leo created the first animated series ever produced in Central America, and founded Rocket Cartoons, one of the most successful animation studios in Latin America. He is also the 2018 winner of the Central American Graphic Novel contest.

I was born in New Mexico.
It was 1930.

I am Mexican American.

I moved to California.

I was treated unfairly because I was Hispanic.

I became a teacher. My students' families worked on farms.

My students did, too.

Farm workers were not treated fairly. I wanted to help. I became a labor leader.

I was an **activist**.

How do you help your community?

I worked with others.
We formed a **union**. We
organized workers. We said,
"Sí, se puede!"

It is like saying, "Yes, we can!"
or "Yes, it can be done!"

We joined with another union.
We organized a strike.

Workers stopped picking grapes.

The strike worked! Workers got paid more. They got **benefits**. Laws changed. I did not stop.

I kept working.

What laws would you change?

I worked for women's rights.
I worked to help **immigrants**.
I worked to help people
in poverty.

I started a **foundation**.

I was awarded the Presidential Medal of Freedom in 2012.

My work inspires people.

What would you like to ask me?

1966

1920

Born
1930

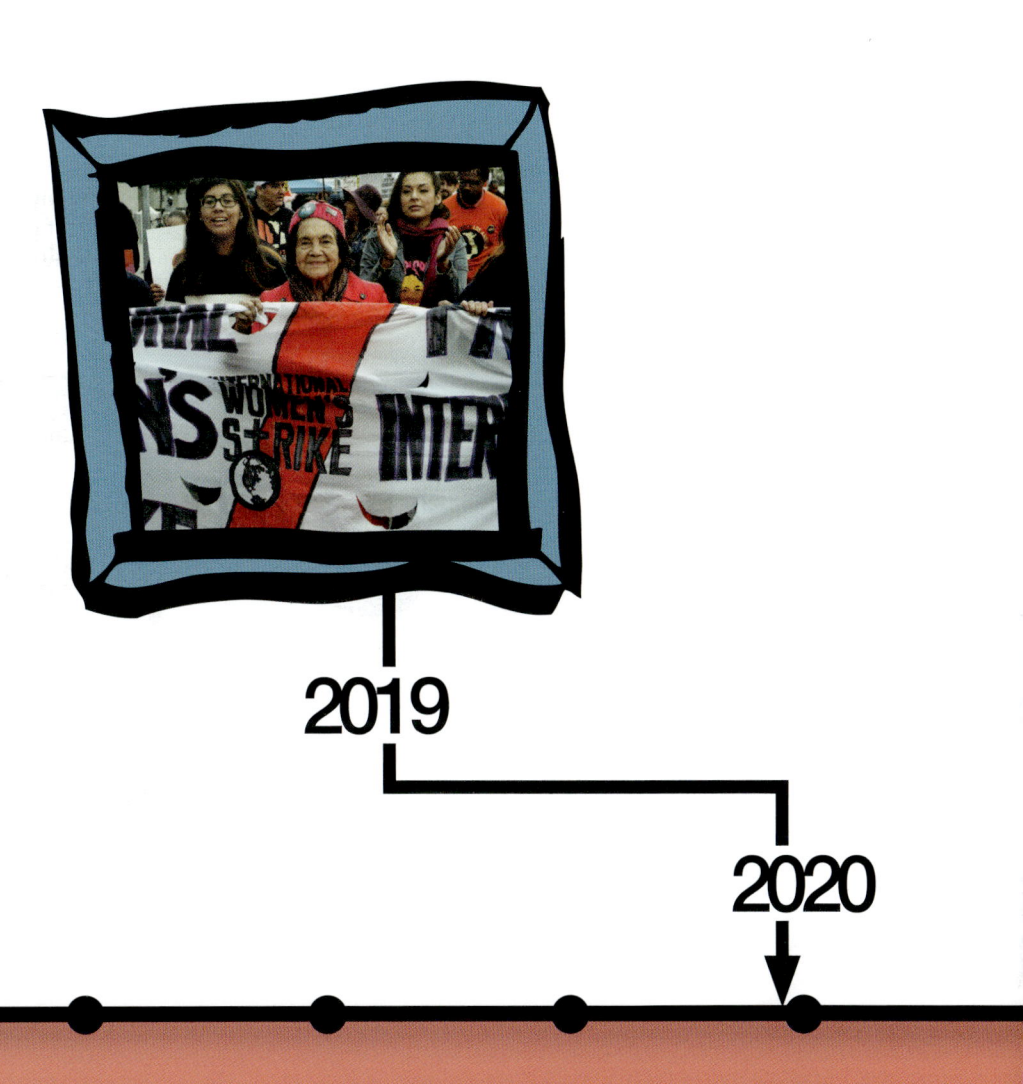

2019

2020

glossary

activist (AK-tih-vist) a person who takes action to support a cause or idea

benefits (BEH-nuh-fits) services or rights employers provide to workers in addition to pay

foundation (fown-DAY-shuhn) an organization set up to support specific causes or goals

immigrants (IH-muh-gruhnts) people who move to one country from another country

union (YOON-yuhn) an organized group of people that works for better pay and fair treatment for its members

index